John Hall Gladstone

Object Teaching

A Lecture

John Hall Gladstone

Object Teaching
 A Lecture

ISBN/EAN: 9783337004712

Printed in Europe, USA, Canada, Australia, Japan

Cover: Foto ©Thomas Meinert / pixelio.de

More available books at **www.hansebooks.com**

OBJECT TEACHING.

A LECTURE.

By J. H. GLADSTONE, Ph.D., F.R.S.

MEMBER OF THE LONDON SCHOOL BOARD.

WITH AN APPENDIX
ON THE USE OF THE BOX OF APPARATUS.

NEW YORK AND CHICAGO:

E. L. KELLOGG & CO.

1888.

OBJECT TEACHING.

OBJECT lessons, as a part of school teaching, owe their origin to an ancient book and to a little boy. The ancient book is the *Orbis Pictus* of that great educational reformer, Comenius. This book had a wonderful sale throughout Germany, and was translated into many languages. In it was started, I believe, the idea of this kind of teaching. The little boy was a scholar of Pestalozzi's school, in which this book was being used.* When they came to the picture of a ladder, the little boy said that there was a real ladder out in the garden, and they might bring it in. The teacher said that would be very troublesome, so he was content with the picture. But on another day they were talking about a window, and the same little boy, who was not to be put down so easily, said that there was a window already in the schoolroom, that had not to be brought in at all, and which they might very easily see; but still the teacher would not take the real window, but only the picture of it. At a meeting of

Origin of object lessons.

---

*This story is told as I first heard it narrated, but various versions of it exist.

the teachers afterwards he mentioned the circumstance, and it was agreed that it was better to talk about the real things themselves; so Pestalozzi was the first to adopt a plan which has since been widely extended. Comenius laid down the principle that children must be taught, as far as possible, not from books, but "from heaven and earth, from oaks and from beeches"; but his book of course contains only the pictures of these things. Then again, it is a book from which Latin could be easily taught; and as it was useful for that purpose, the higher purpose of teaching from real things was to a great extent lost sight of. Pestalozzi tried to follow the order of nature, and held that the end of education was the harmonious development of all the natural powers and faculties of the mind. He held that what is to be known must first be perceived by the senses. But, after all, the object lessons which Pestalozzi introduced were not very good. He was the beginner only. He often thought much more about the memory than about the intelligence, and made his scholars repeat names or sentences many times over without explaining anything about them. However, the intuitional method of teaching was started. I use the word "intuitional" because I do not know a better translation of *Anschauungs-Unterricht*, which was the expression that Pestalozzi used.* He meant that teaching was to be by means of the senses—we were

---

* The same word is adopted by M. Buisson, Inspector-General of Public Instruction in France, to whose admirable *Conférence sur l'Enseignement Intuitif* I am indebted for many thoughts in this lecture.

first to get hold of something we could hear, or feel, or see, or taste, and, having acquired such perceptions of the thing itself, they were to be the foundation of our knowledge. That being the method of teaching used at home and in the nursery, he held that it ought also to be adopted in the schools.

This intuitional method of teaching came over into England. I need hardly tell you that in the old English schools there were no object lessons at all. In those parochial schools that were started *Adopted in England after 1839.* during the past century all over England, they thought nothing whatever about science; and indeed, at the commencement of the operations of the National Society, and of the British and Foreign School Society, little was cared about natural knowledge. In the training colleges it was not taught. The Home and Colonial Training College paid a good deal of attention, even in its earlier years, to natural history; and in their Model School they sought " through visible objects and questions to cultivate the senses of the children, and to give a practical tendency to all they acquired." This was in 1839. Afterwards the Home and Colonial Society produced various works on the subject, and obtained a pre-eminence for this kind of teaching through the senses.

But although this method of teaching by means of the natural objects themselves came rather rapidly into use in our element- *It becomes mechanical.* ary schools, two great misfortunes happened. The first was that it became very mechanical or artificial. Now, the very object, the first

requisite of such teaching is, that it shall be as free
and as natural as nature itself; that there shall be
all the variety which we find round about us in the
universe, without the stiffness which we have in our
own artificial arrangements.   Do you know what the
difference is?   **If you** compare natural with artificial
flowers, you will find a good deal of difference between **them.**   But I will give you another illustration.
What do we do in our decorations?   We have no
wall papers or plaster cornices in this room, but you
can easily imagine them in your mind.   In all prob-
ability, if there were, flowers would be introduced.
But **what** sort of flowers?   They would be of con-
ventional form: not the forms we find in nature, but
something much more stiff and much more regular.
Then again, in the case of the wall paper, they would
be repeated at equal distances.   If we had a plaster
moulding there might be flowers too, but depend
upon it they would be marvelously symmetrical, and
would be repeated over and over again along the
whole length of the cornice.   That is man's way of
working.   The highest attempt of mechanical art is
to make these regular forms, and to repeat them.

But nature has a different way of working.   The
flowers she produces are all different
one from another, even those of the
same species.   No two leaves of the
same tree **are** exactly alike.   There is unity running
through the whole, unity of purpose, unity of general form, unity of design; but there is also diversity.
This diversity we ought to have in all our teaching.
There should be no artificial lessons.   If you look

It should be free
and natural.

at some of the books in which object lessons are taught, you will find a whole string of properties put down; then on the next page, it may be, for some other object, another long string of properties, in very much the same order, and running through the same set of ideas. But a child does not think of all the qualities of a thing, and catalogue them in his own mind. That is not a child's way of beginning. The human mind certainly never works in that way, even in grown up people. In a well-known book, a key, a knife, an orange, a buttercup, and a lady-bird, are all described as being opaque, and the teacher is expected, in giving a lesson on any of these objects, to write on the blackboard, o-p-a-q-u-e. That is an instance of the artificiality which came in to so large an extent, and injured the good cause. Lessons of this character are of course not educational, and young teachers are apt to get hold of the faults of these books instead of their excellencies, and to harden and petrify the lessons till they give their children a stone instead of bread.

The other misfortune was this. By the revised code of 1861 object teaching was to a large extent banished from the schools. The books just mentioned were thrown aside ; the collections of things be-

Object teaching discarded for a time.

came dusty and **went** to pieces ; the diagrams became dirty ; and all attention was given to reading, writing, and arithmetic — I do not say whether rightly or wrongly at that time. There may have been good reasons for it ; that I have nothing to do with just now ; but at any rate that was the fact. Intuitional

teaching was not paid for, and it was almost discarded from the schools. It remained in many of
the infant schools, but there was very little of this
sympathetic knowledge of nature in the teaching
that was then given in our boys' or girls' schools. It
is true that there was always a great outcry against
its cessation. The utilitarians said it was much more
important to teach children things that they could
actually make use of in after life, knowledge which
would be serviceable to them in their business ; that,
in fact, it was better that they should know the different parts and functions of their body, than how many
mountains there might be in Tartary, or the precise
length of the Mississippi or the Danube. Then again
there were the advocates of science. They claimed
that as science was rising to be such an important
power in the country, it was an absurdity and a
shame to shut it out of our public schools ; that to
keep children from the study of science, and to limit
them to books and to words embodying simply
human ideas, was ridiculous, and was doing a wrong
to the whole rising generation. Then again, the
educational reformers joined in the same cry, argu-
ing that this kind of teaching developed certain of
the faculties, for instance, the faculties of observation
and perception, which could not be devéloped half
so well in any other way. They also claimed that
the judgment ought to be cultivated, and that it could
be better educated upon things than upon words.
This controversy went on for some considerable time;
but so far as the code was concerned object lessons
did not appear at all, and if they were given in the

schools they were ignored by Her Majesty's Inspector, and not rewarded by any grant. Some of
the more developed sciences, however, came in re-
cently under the name of "specific subjects."

It was, I believe, the code of 1880 which acknowl-
edged, for the first time, the existence
of object lessons ; and then only with   **Again in the
schools.**
reference to infant schools ; but there
was no grant given for them. This code also arranged that there might be a continuation from these
object lessons through all standards above the first,
and that such subjects as Natural History or Natural Philosophy might be taken as class subjects.
So far so good ; it was a sign of better things coming. But now, in the present code of 1882, we have
a different state of affairs. I dare say you are aware
that under the heading of " Infant schools " not only
is object teaching mentioned, but it is put in the
right place, not in a note, but in the body of the code.
It provides also that in the case of infant schools the
merit grant is contingent, among other things, on
there being " simple lessons on objects and on the
phenomena of nature and of common life "; and
although this applies only to the infant schools, still
the code makes provision that in the first standard
and upwards there may be taken as class subjects,
geography, physical as well as political, or elementary
science. You are aware that our London Board has
laid it down from the commencement, that object
lessons should be taught not only in the infant schools,
but in the boys' and girls' departments, and that
they should lead up to more scientific teaching. A

detailed scheme of object teaching, and instructions for carrying it out, were drawn up some years ago and printed as a circular. Of course, what with the encouragement which the School Board gives, and the remuneration which the Government gives, and the increasing knowledge of these subjects, and the efforts of educational reformers, I have no doubt that this intuitional method of teaching will find its way much more fully into our schools.

Now, what ought object lessons to be? First, in regard to the time-table — When **When should object lessons be given?** ought they to be taken up? Should it be near the end of the day? I think not. I think that they require the full strength of our senses, and of our minds, and of our reasoning powers ; so they ought to be taken up at some time when our faculties are fresh. There are other subjects, you know, which do not make such a strain upon the mind, drawing, singing, needlework, and other things of that sort, which may form a kind of rest after the more strenuous work.

I would say to all teachers — Choose your object **What subjects?** carefully beforehand. It should be something that is within the comprehension of a child, but which the child does not fully understand already. If it is something familiar to them, so much the better. Or you may choose, if you like, several objects, having some property in common ; for instance, you may take a sponge, a piece of sugar, a piece of flannel, and a brick, all of which things, though they differ greatly from one another, agree in being porous, that is to say, they will soak up water. Or you may take things which have several qualities in common, and get the children to observe the differences. You might ask your children, for instance, to bring you leaves from as many kinds of trees as they can — the fir tree, apple tree, maple, poplar, oak, and various others, and note in what they differ. If you have to deal with very young children your lessons may be very miscellaneous ; **but, as the** children become older, more order **and** sequence **may be** expected in the subjects chosen ; and indeed the object lessons will gradually **merge** into the systematic scheme of " elementary **science** " contemplated in the new code.

Having chosen your object or objects, you must study them well beforehand. Now, what are you going to study them for ? Are you going to study them in order to see how much you can say about them ? If so, you are not doing the best thing. What I want you to do is, to study your object with this purpose— **that you** may see how much you can make the object itself tell. You want the object to speak, rather than yourself. You ought to put an object before the children in such a way that they may understand and learn lessons from it, not that you should talk about it and introduce information gathered from I know not where.

Object must be studied.

Before you begin, get a good supply of the object or objects. You may have these already in the school, or you may have to get a quantity. If it be the leaves of different trees, ask your scholars to bring such

Get the object or pictures.

leaves as they can. It may be that you cannot get
the objects themselves, because of course it is evident
that there are some things which you cannot bring
into the school, such as a lion or a volcano. In that
case the best thing you can do is to get a good picture of them — a picture properly colored. Perhaps
sometimes you may make an explanatory diagram,
or a drawing on the blackboard, which I should
advise you always to have beside you when giving
object lessons.

Having the objects, you must not only make your
How to use the object. scholars look at them, but you must
make them see. That is quite another
thing, is it not? It is possible to show
a great many things to children without making them
see, and feel, and understand them. Make them
observe and remember what they perceive with their
fingers, or eyes, or nose, or tongue. I do not care
which. of their senses may be appealed to. Drop
your object on the floor ; do various things with it.
Try to make your scholars find out all they can
about the objects ; help them to think about them
and talk about them ; find out what they know in the
first instance, and then of course you may help them
slowly to discover a great many other things. Do
not of course dwell upon points which they know
very well, but take care that they understand everything as you proceed. Sometimes I have seen almost
the exactly opposite thing done. I recollect, for instance, seeing an object lesson given upon glass.
The term " brittle " had been used, the teacher having stated that glass was brittle, and the word

"brittle" was written upon the blackboard in the proper orthodox form. Yes; the children were told that glass was brittle. I rather think that most of them had already learned by experience that glass could be broken easily; but they did not know that glass was "brittle," because, when the mistress and I began to examine the class, we found that very few of them knew what the word brittle meant. If you choose to say to your pupils that things which can be easily broken are called brittle, then you give them the use of another word. But you may use words of which they have no conception at all, and they may repeat the words to you; and you may think they understand because they use the words quite correctly.

I have been told of a gentleman who used to teach science in schools; my friend who knew him did not approve of his method, and said so, and was invited to come and witness it in operation; **Words used must be comprehended.** whereupon he paid a visit to the school, and the teacher said, "Here you can have botany, astronomy, physiology, or anything else. What would you like to ask my class about?" "Well," said the visitor, "I would rather you asked them yourself. Suppose you take the solar system?" "Yes, certainly," was the reply, and a diagram of the solar system was hung up, and on his pointing to different things his pupils explained the figure in the center as the sun, the positions of Mercury and Venus, and so on. When he pointed to a particular circle, they explained that that was the orbit of Venus. The whole thing was gone through in a very satisfactory way, and they gave pat answers to the questions of the teacher. The visitor then offered to put a few questions. He began by asking, "What is an orbit?" None of them knew. They had used the word orbit, but they did not know what an orbit was. "But," he continued, "cannot you give me something near it? Give us an idea of what an orbit is. Is it a coal-scuttle, or a flower-pot?" One little boy said, "A coal-scuttle, sir." As that was not right, of course the rest of the class joined in saying that it was a flower-pot. Mind you do not use words that the children do not understand, and because they repeat them to you, think that therefore you have got the idea itself into their heads.

As to definitions, some teachers are content with giving definitions of their own.

Pupils make definitions. Rather get your scholars to make the definitions for themselves, working them out so that they shall understand them. Do not begin by giving a definition—even grown-up people do not like that. We do not think of what is abstract first of all, we think of what is concrete, and then we build up our more general ideas; and with children this is still more the case. Let them form an idea of what porosity is by examining a number of things, all of which are porous, instead of your giving a definition and expecting the class to repeat it two or three times. In the latter case, when you ask, What is porosity? your class gives it out, of course, in exactly the words which you have used. You may think it all very nice because they give the definition in precisely the form in **which it** was taught to them. Now, I always suspect such cases. If your children repeat your definitions in **the** same words that you have given them, suspect at **once** that there is something wrong in your teaching. **If you** have made them understand the subject, their **words** will almost certainly be somewhat different from your own, perhaps less exact and more colloquial, but showing **that they** have a real idea in **their** minds.

In carrying out this line of instruction you should use all the appliances you can. **You must use the** blackboard, as I **have said** before, and make any drawings **Make drawings when needed.** that will illustrate the subject. Such impromptu sketches would be very valuable, for instance, if you were talking about leaves. There are various things about the room which you may press into your service. The fire will come in useful if you want to show whether a thing will burn or not. If you are **giving** lessons upon mechanical forces, you do not **want** any elaborate apparatus; you may take any ordinary stick or wooden lath, and make a great many **useful** and valuable experiments with it.

I listened the other day to a teacher **giving** a lesson upon the inclined plane. He began by asking his class if they **had** **Lesson on an inclined plane.** seen a sugar hogshead being **taken** into a grocer's shop, and had noticed what was done when it came to the step. They began to think **about it, and** some of them remembered that planks were put up upon the steps, and that if the planks

were too steep they had to be put out at greater
length so as to make the slope easier.   Then he asked
what was the meaning of that, and so he led them
on to know something of the inclined plane; and
he had his own model of the inclined plane, made
by his own hands, and he gave a lesson from that.
It happened to be a rather advanced class, so he could
go a little into the mathematics of the question.
Of course, so far as the arithmetic was concerned, it
was extremely simple, but it was really scientific.

The School Board has arranged that every teacher
who requisitions it, should have a little box of apparatus like this which I have here.   It contains test-
tubes and various other things of which you may
advantageously make use.   I will now show you one
or two simple experiments by means of them.

Supposing you were to take that very common
substance, water, and talk about it;

Lesson on water.

you could do so to almost any extent,
I suppose.   You might show how wa-
ter wets some bodies and does not wet others.   You
could show too that you cannot pick up a quantity
of water, but only a drop or two at a time; that you
can pour out water, and so on.   Possibly your class
will tell you that water will dissolve things.   Well,
ask them what they mean by dissolving.   Possibly
you may find that they have no very clear notion of
what becomes of a thing when it is dissolved; and
you may show them that.   In order to use the apparatus I will first dissolve a little salt in water, and
show how the salt may be brought back again.   You
may like to spend a little time over it, and see the

salt gradually disappear, or you may do it more quickly by warming the water over the lamp. If you want to dissolve it in a test-tube, you must warm the glass as I am doing, below the surface of the liquid, or you will run a good chance of cracking it. You see that the salt is very rapidly disappearing; it is now almost all gone. When it is all dissolved, you can show your class that the water is perfectly clear, they can see no salt whatever. Well, what has become of it ? I do not know that it would be a bad way of carrying out this intuitional method of instruction by making them taste it, so that they will get the information by one sense if not by another. We can get back the salt by boiling off the water. If you take a little basin and put the lamp under it, you will soon boil away the water, and, as you will see, the salt will crystallize out and remain behind. That will be an interesting experiment to your little people. While the water is being evaporated away, you may draw your class's attention to the steam going up into the atmosphere ; and if you have any cold substance, you may condense some of the steam upon it. A piece of glass or a slate will answer the purpose. You may then carry the illustration a little further, and show that your breath frequently condenses upon the windows. In the morning when you rise up, if it has been cold during the night, you find that the windows are covered with condensed water, which is simply the steam from your lungs. If there has been a frost outside, this steam, instead of being water, will be frozen into ice. And so you may lead on from these little experiments that you

make in your school-room, right up to the great
phenomena of nature, clouds, rain, hail, and snow.

Here is the salt which has been reproduced by the
boiling off of the water—back again just as it was
before, with all its properties unchanged.

I should like to show you the whole process of
boiling water. Few of the children
Lesson on boil- have ever seen it; they have seen
ing water. what is called "the kettle boiling," but
the water was inside, and at most they could see the
bubbles on the top of it, and the steam coming out
of the spout. You do not see what is going on unless you use a transparent vessel. I will pour some
water into this large glass test-tube and heat it over
the lamp. You will see, first of all, that directly I
warm it, there is a certain amount of air given off.
These first small bubbles are not steam, but air. As
the water begins to boil at the bottom, you will see
bubbles of steam form, and as they are condensed by
the colder water above, they make the gurgling sort
of sound which you hear. That is the cause of the
singing noise which is heard in the kettle. Now the
bubbles rise higher and higher, till at last they burst
on the surface, and the liquid is boiling throughout,
and the steam is going off into the air. I have no
time now to show you the uses of the other pieces
of apparatus, or of the magnifying glass; but I will
explain them to any of you who may come to me
after the lecture.

But I want to show you a more excellent way of
teaching. If I were a school-master or school-mis-
tress, and could have my own way quite irrespective

of all regulations, I do not know that I should have
any set time for object lessons at all.
I should have regular time for science
lessons no doubt, but I am not sure
whether I should have even that in
case of young children up to nine

Object teaching
to form the
basis of all
teaching.

or ten years of age. I would rather have this object
teaching to form the basis of all the instruction that
is given throughout the school. I would have it as
a sort of leaven, which is to raise the whole body of
studies, and make it light and wholesome. I should
like to give it for the purpose of bringing the minds
of the children into contact with nature in every
direction, a sort of network between their thoughts
and the universe around, whether it be in what is
called object lessons or science lessons, because the
one passes insensibly into the other. And, in order
that there may be this kind of intuitional teaching
running through the whole of our work, certain
things are requisite.

First of all the teacher must have a general knowledge of and sympathy with nature.
It is by no means necessary that the
teachers should be scientific men or
scientific women; but they should

Sympathy with
nature a requi-
site.

have their eyes open to the beauties of the universe
around, and they should know something about it.
I want that there should be more of this knowledge
among the teachers connected with our schools; and
hence in these pupil teachers' centers we want that
the teaching shall be not so much of high sciences, as of those fundamental principles which un-

derlie the whole of science, so that you shall be able
to recognize what is going on in nature round about
you; and shall have that sort of knowledge which
will fit you for taking up chemistry, or physiology,
or botany, or anything else afterwards. I know Mr.
Cox and Mr. Gordon could explain to you a great
many advanced sciences, if they chose to do so; but,
I repeat, what we want to be taught here, is not so
much these advanced matters as those principles
which will lead you easily to take up the special sciences, if you choose to do so eventually. And so
we wish you to acquire some knowledge of the ani-
mal world, of the vegetable world, of the mineral
world, of the forces of nature, the mechanical powers,
and so on; and that you may get this knowledge
thoroughly into your minds, so that you may use it
afterwards in teaching, or for your own further studies, we propose to teach here physiography, so that
you may take a South Kensington certificate in that
science, if you like, and with a little more prepara-
tion you may take chemistry, geology, and many
other subjects. What we most want is this general
sympathy with nature, and knowledge of it. You
must not only have this in your minds, but you must
have also an assortment of objects to work with.

You should have something like a school museum.
As you are aware, the School Board
will supply you with a number of
objects, but it is much better if you
can get your children to bring you
objects, and thus get together a nice little collection.
The school museum is useful in two ways,— the

A school
museum
needed.

gathering of the various things creates an interest in the little people themselves, and is itself very instructive ; and when you have got a fair collection, then, of course, it is ready for use at any time. I have seen splendid collections in some of our schools — one collection illustrating the whole of the geology of the neighborhood, another containing the bones of many different animals, and the various spices and products from distant lands. Your children will have a great many different tastes, and will bring a great variety of things. Well, take these things and put them into your museum, if they are worth it ; and you will find it a great incentive if you put upon a label the name of the little person who brings anything good.

But, you will say, where is this museum to be kept ? The School Board will supply a cabinet to every teacher who shows that he has a sufficiently fair collection, and that he is desirous of keeping the things in proper order. Henceforth I hope to find these cabinets not only in the schools of the Chelsea division, but in the schools all over London.

Now, an object lesson may be introduced in the course of the reading lesson, or whatever it may be, and need not occupy more than two minutes. You can go to the cabinet, and take out something *Suggestions as to lessons on objects.* which illustrates the passage which is being read. In this way the scripture lesson, or history, may be rendered more vivid and truthful ; and the illustrations by real objects will give an interest to the lessons in the eyes of the children. And there may be not only lessons upon particular subjects, but you may take advantage also of the bright sunshine such as is coming into this room to-day. You may have a prism and show, as you can easily do, how the light may be split up into different colored rays upon the white walls of the room. You are required by the code to give lessons on the different phenomena of nature, such as rain, hail, frost, etc. Just take an opportunity of speaking about them when they occur, not when they do not occur, so that the children may actually see them ; and interrupt their ordinary lessons — at least I should like to do so — for the purpose of talking about these things. There are phenomena which do not frequently occur ; take advantage of them when they do come — a thunderstorm, for instance. Then you may make your children see the grandeur of the heavens ; call attention to the flashing lightning and the pealing thunder. I do not know exactly what you might care to teach about them to very young children, but if they are more advanced, and know anything of science, you can teach them much. At any rate, you can make them feel what you are feeling, that it is grand and sublime, and draw them on to higher and better thoughts. If you speak in the right tone, they will remember what you say for a long time afterwards, and perhaps they will think all the more of you because they will know you as something far better than a mere teacher of arithmetic or grammar. In the same way you may take advantage of any public events, or anything happening in the locality, and draw lessons from them.

There are also permanent experiments that may be carried on in the schools; for instance, plants, such as hyacinths, may be grown, and horse-chestnuts, and

Experiments in school-room.

others, which you can see putting out their little roots and leaves. Such things, you will find, will be watched with great interest. In one of our schools there is an aquarium. It is interesting to observe the little creatures that are there : such a thing as the development of a tadpole into a frog would be very interesting. Then there is the keeping of silk-worms, and many other things, all of which are very attractive, and will quicken the perceptions of the little observers. They will bring you and your scholars into closer sympathy with one another too.

Of course, working under the code, we must have object lessons upon the time table in the infant schools—there is no doubt about that ; and in the upper **departments** science will make its appearance under some other form. But beyond the set lessons I would bring before the children, from time to time, informal ones as occasion may arise. I have a strong belief that you will find it well to infuse this kind of teaching into the whole of your instruction, and to weld the whole together as much as possible by that means, so that this education may go on gradually extending more and more into a scientific manner of working and thinking. In learning specific subjects, and in any technical pursuits which your children may turn to in after life, this groundwork will be of immense value, and it will also be of service as far as home life is concerned. It will assist

them in their domestic affairs, and even in the lighting of fires, and cooking, better than any amount of
abstract knowledge could do; and in the different
trades and industries to which they may turn they
will succeed much better for having some knowledge
of the first principles of nature. Thus also you will
give them an interest in all that is around them,
they will have opportunities and sources of enjoy-
ment **opened to** them, which will keep them from
many of the low and debasing pleasures to which
they might otherwise become addicted; and they
will acquire a taste for studies of an elevating character, which will become a beauty and a source of
strength to them all through life.

APPENDIX.

ON THE USE OF THE BOX OF APPARATUS.

The small box of apparatus used by the London
School Board consists of thirty-four different arti-
cles :—

The *knife*, *saw*, and *file* are tools so well known that
it is unnecessary to explain their various uses.

The *spirit lamp* is intended for showing the action
of heat upon objects. When the wick is ignited the
flame can be regulated by pulling the wick further
out, or pushing it in, by means of a *wire*.

In order to burn or heat solid bodies in this flame
they may be supported on a *bent wire*, or the *wire*

tripod, or an ordinary shovel or tongs may be used. Solids may be melted in one of the *tin basins, watch-glasses*, or *test-tubes*. Liquids also may be boiled, or solutions may be made, in any of these.

In order to heat anything in the *tin basin* it is merely necessary to support it on the *wire tripod*, and place the spirit lamp underneath. The substance to be heated should be placed in the *basin* before the lamp is applied.

In order to heat anything in a *test-tube*, it is necessary to hold a tube near the open end, by means of the *wooden tongs*, as shown in the diagram, or between the forefinger and thumb in the same position.* The flame should play only on the lower part of the tube, or the tube should be held above it, according to the heat required. After the *test-tube* has been used it should be well rinsed with water. A test-tube with liquid in it may be safely stood in a wooden *block with holes*.

With this apparatus it will be easy to show that a variety of bodies, as, for instance, straw, orange peel, or iron filings, will burn, and to call attention to the phenomena of their combustion; or, on the other hand, to show that others will not burn, as, for instance, salt, flint, or silver. Again, that other solids, as ice, rosin, or sugar, will melt; and most liquids, as water, spirits of wine, or turpentine, will boil and go off in vapor.

On heating water in a test-tube, there will be ob-

---

* The open end should always be held away from the person, in case the contents should suddenly shoot out of the tube.

served, first, the separation of minute bubbles of
atmospheric air; then currents produced by the dif-
ferently-heated strata of liquid; afterwards the formation of large bubbles of steam against the hot glass,
condensing with a peculiar noise as they rise into
the cooler water, followed by the gradual ebullition
of the whole liquid, the bubbles breaking on the
surface and the steam rising into the tube. The
steam condenses at first in the upper part of the tube,
but afterwards passes into the air and may be condensed in another tube or on any cold surface. In
boiling combustible liquids, such as spirits of wine
and turpentine, care must be taken that they do not
boil over and so catch fire. Some solid volatile
bodies, such as camphor, may be melted in a test-
tube, and the vapors will condense in the upper part
of the tube as bright little crystals: these may be
examined with advantage with a *magnifying glass*.

With this apparatus also many substances, such as
salt, sugar, or gum, may be dissolved in water; others
such as lard, shellac, or camphor, will dissolve in
spirits. This process of solution will be expedited
by stirring, for which purpose a slate pencil can be
used. The actual presence of colorless substances
in the liquid may often be recognized by the taste
or smell, though not by the sight: but colored bodies, such as sulphate of copper, cochineal, or laun-
dresses' blue, reveal their presence in the solution by
their color. The substance dissolved may be recov-
ered by evaporating off the water or spirit; this may
be best done in one of the *basins;* the liquid may be
boiled freely at first, but when the solid substance be-

gins to separate it should be heated more gently. In such cases as sulphate of copper, alum, niter, etc., if, when the solution is nearly evaporated down, the liquid be allowed to cool, crystals of the previously dissolved substance will make their appearance; they will disappear again on warming the liquid.

Permanent changes may also be produced by heat: thus crystals of soda will lose the water they contain, and fall into **powder**. **Starch** will not be dissolved by cold water, but on heating the liquid it will disappear, and on cooling it will not separate into grains as before, but will form a jelly. The hardening by heat (coagulation) of white of egg, or of raw meat, may be rendered visible, with or without the aid of water.

Many substances such as coffee, or peruvian bark, are made up of both soluble and insoluble bodies. These may be separated by letting them soak in water, and **filtering them**. To form a *filter* take one of the round papers, fold it in half and then into quarters: then open it with the finger so that three thicknesses **of** the paper shall be on one side and **one on** the other. This will form a hollow cone, which will fit exactly into the glass funnel. Wet the paper filter with water, and then pour the mixture into it; the insoluble part will remain on the paper, while the soluble portion will fall into a testtube or any other vessel placed below to receive it. The difference between solution and mere suspension in water may be shown by ink, which of course will pass through **such a** filter, and black lead mixed up with water, which will be retained by the paper.

The narrow *glass tubes* may be used for conveying gases and liquids, and illustrating many of the mechanical laws to which these forms of matter are subject. Thus a tube just dipped into water and drawn out again will hold a small quantity of water by capillary attraction; or if the finger be placed tightly upon the open end a much larger quantity may be lifted up in consequence of the pressure of the atmosphere. An instructive experiment may be made by breathing through one of these tubes into lime water, when the carbonic acid of the breath will become evident by the formation of white carbonate of lime, which will make the water milky. The *bent glass tube* will act either as a syphon, or as a means of showing that water will find its level.

A *glass tube* may be bent when strongly heated in the flame of the spirit lamp; or it can be neatly broken across if a notch be first cut in it with the *triangular file*.

The *tobacco pipe* may be used for blowing bubbles, and thus showing some of the mechanical and optical properties of thin films of liquid; or for the common experiment of roasting a piece of coal in the bowl of the pipe, stopped up with clay, and lighting the gas as it issues through the mouthpiece.

The *litmus paper* will be useful in more strictly chemical experiments by distinguishing between acid substances, such as vinegar, orange juice, or hydrochloric acid gas, which turn it red; and alkaline substances, such as soda, lime water, and ammonia gas, which turn it blue.

The *magnifying glass* will be useful for examining

the structure of any small bodies, such as insects, corals, and the minute parts of flowers, etc. These may be laid upon a card, and the glass stood over them resting upon the brass rim. A watch glass may be employed if liquids are examined or light underneath is desired. The small tools accompanying the *magnifying glass* are intended for holding or taking to pieces the different objects.

In addition to the above uses of these pieces of apparatus each one of them itself might form an object lesson. Thus attention could be drawn to the different materials which go to form the *clasp knife, spirit lamp,* and *magnifying glass;* and their adaptation to their purposes. The different mode of action of the *knife, saw,* and *file* might be demonstrated. The flame of the *spirit lamp* also might be the starting point for lessons on light as well as heat.

BOOKS FOR TEACHERS.

Love's Industrial Education.

Industrial Education ; a guide to Manual Training. By
SAMUEL G. LOVE, principal of the Jamestown, (N. Y.)
public schools. Cloth, 12mo, 330 pp. with 40 full-page
plates containing nearly 400 figures. Price, $1.75 ; *to
teachers*, $1.40 ; by mail, 12 cents extra.

1. *Industrial Education not understood.* Probably the only
man who has wrought out the problem in a practical way is
Samuel G. Love, the superin-
tendent of the Jamestown (N.
Y.) schools. Mr. Love has now
about 2,400 children in the
primary, advanced, and high
schools under his charge ; he
is assisted by fifty teachers, so
that an admirable opportunity
was offered. In 1874 (about
fourteen years ago) Mr. Love
began his experiment ; gradually he introduced one occu-
pation, and then another, until
at last nearly all the pupils are
following some form of educat-
ing work.

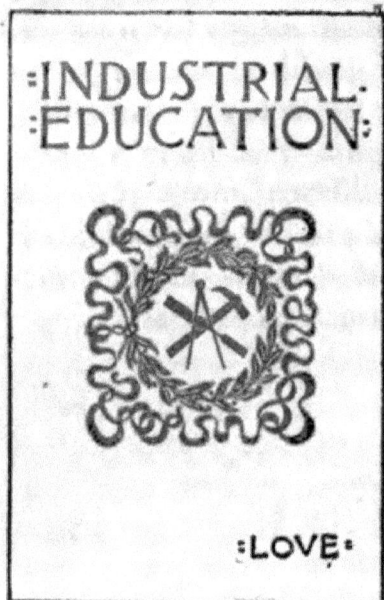

2. *Why it is demanded.* The
reasons for introducing it are
clearly stated by Mr. Love. It
was done because the education of the books left the pupils unfitted to meet the prac-
tical problems the world asks them to solve. The world does
not have a field ready for the student in book-lore. The state-
ments of Mr. Love should be carefully read.

3. *It is an educational book.* Any one can give some
formal work to girls and boys. What has been needed has
been some one who could find out what is suited to the little
child who is in the " First Reader," to the one who is in the
"Second Reader," and so on. It must be remembered the
effort is not to make carpenters, and type-setters, and dress-
makers of boys and girls, but to *educate them by these occupations better than without them.*

4. *It tells the teacher just what to do.* Every teacher should put **some** form of Manual Training into his school. At present the only **ones** are Gymnastics, Writing, and Drawing. But there are, it is estimated, more than thirty forms of Industrial Work that may be made *educative.* The teacher who studies this book will want to try some of these forms. He will find light on the subject.

5. *It must be noted that a demand now exists for men and women to give Industrial Training.* Those teachers who are **wise** will begin now to study this important subject. The city of New York has decided to introduce it into its schools, where 140,000 pupils are gathered. It is a mighty undertaking, but it will succeed. The people see the need of a different education than that given by the books. Book education is faulty, partial, incomplete. But where are the men and women to come from who can give instruction? Those who read this book and set to work to introduce its methods into their schools will be fitting themselves for higher positions.

The **Lutheran Observer** says:—" This volume on Manual Teaching ought to be speedily introduced into all the public schools. It is admirably adapted for its purpose and we recommend it to teachers everywhere."

The **Nashville American** says:—"This is a practical volume. It embodies the results of many years of trial in a search after those occupations that will educate in the true sense of the word. It is not a work dealing in theories or abstractions, but in methods and details, such as will help the teacher or parent selecting occupations for children."

West Virginia School Journal.—"It shows what can be done **by a** resolute and spirited teacher."

Burlington Free Press.—" An excellent hand book."

Prin. Sherman Williams, Glens Falls, N. Y.—"I am **sure it will** greatly aid the solution of this difficult problem."

Prof. Edward Brooks, Late Principal Millersburg, (Pa.) Normal School.—" It is a much needed work; is the best book I have seen."

Supt. S. T. Dutton, New Haven.—"The book is proof that some practical results have been reached and is full of promise for the future.

Supt. John E. Bodley, Minneapolis.—"I know of no one more competent to tell other superintendents and teachers how to introduce Manual Training than Prof. Love."

Oil City Blizzard.—"The system he has marked out must be a good one, or he would never have allowed it to go out."

Buffalo Times.—" Teachers are looking into this subject and this will help them."

Boston Advertiser.—" A plain unvarnished explanation."

Jamestown, N. Y. Evening Journal.—" In the hands of an intelligent teacher cannot fail to yield satisfactory results."

Currie's Early Education.

" The Principles and Practice of Early and Infant School Education." By JAMES CURRIE, A. M., Prin. Church of Scotland Training College, Edinburgh. Author of " Common School Education," etc. With an introduction by Clarence E. Meleney, A. M., Supt. Schools, Paterson, N. J. Bound in blue cloth, gold, 16mo, 290 pp. Price, $1.25 ; *to teachers,* $1.00 ; by mail, 8 cents extra.

WHY THIS BOOK IS VALUABLE.

1. Pestalozzi gave New England its educational supremacy. The Pestalozzian wave struck this country more than forty years ago, and produced a mighty shock. It set New England to thinking. Horace Mann became eloquent to help on the change, and went up and down Massachusetts, urging in earnest tones the change proposed by the Swiss educator. What gave New England its educational supremacy was its reception of Pestalozzi's doctrines. Page, Philbrick, Barnard were all his disciples.

2. It is the work of one of the best expounders of Pestalozzi.

Forty years ago there was an upheaval in education. Pestalozzi's words were acting like yeast upon educators ; thousands had been to visit his schools at Yverdun, and on their return to their own lands had reported the wonderful scenes they had witnessed. Rev. James Currie comprehended the movement, and sought to introduce it. Grasping the ideas of this great teacher, he spread them in Scotland ; but that country was not elastic and receptive. Still, Mr. Currie's presentation of them wrought a great change, and he is to be reckoned as the most powerful exponent of the new ideas in Scotland. Hence this book, which contains them, must be considered as a treasure by the educator.

3. This volume is really a Manual of Principles of Teaching. It exhibits enough of the principles to make the teacher intelligent in her practice. Most manuals give details, but no foundation principles. The first part lays a psychological basis—the only one there is for the teacher ; and this is done in a simple and concise way. He declares emphatically that teaching cannot be learned empirically. That is, that one cannot watch a teacher and see *how* he does it, and then, imitating, claim to be a teacher. The principles must be learned.

4. It is a Manual of Practice in Teaching.

It discusses the subjects of Number, Object Lessons, Color, Form, Geography, Singing, and Reading in a most intelligent manner. There is a world of valuable suggestions here for the teacher.

5. It points out the characteristics of Lesson-Giving—or Good Teaching.

The language of the teacher, the tone of voice, the questioning needed, the sympathy with the class, the cheerfulness needed, the patience, the self-possession, the animation, the decorum, the discipline, are all discussed, This latter term is defined, and it needs to be, for most teachers use it to cover all reasons for doing—it is for " discipline " they do everything.

6. It discusses the motives to be used in teaching.

Any one who can throw light here will be listened to ; Mr. Currie has done this admirably. He puts (1) Activity, (2) Love, (3) Social Relation, as the three main motives. Rewards and Punishments, Bribery, etc., are here well treated. The author was evidently a man " ahead of his times ;" everywhere we see the spirit of a humane man ; he is a lover of children, a student of childhood, a deep thinker on subjects that seem very easy to the pretentious pedagogue.

7. The book has an admirable introduction,

By Supt. Meleney, of Paterson, N. J., a disciple of the New Education, and one of the most promising of the new style of educators that are coming to the front in these days. Taking it all together, it is a volume that well deserves wonderful popularity.

Adopted by the Chautauqua Teachers' Reading Union.

Philadelphia Teacher.—" It is a volume that every primary teacher should study."

Boston Common School Education.—" It will prove a **great boon to** thousands of earnest teachers."

Virginia Educational Journal.—" Mr. Currie has **long** been esteemed by educators."

Central School Journal.—" Books like this cannot but hasten the day for a better valuation of childhood."

North Carolina School Teacher.—" An interesting and timely book."

FOR READING CIRCLES.

" Payne's Lectures " is pre-eminently THE book for Reading Circles. It has already been adopted by the New York, Ohio, Philadelphia, New Jersey, Illinois, Colorado, and Chautauqua Circles, besides many in counties and cities. *Remember that our edition is far superior to any other published.*

Shaw's National Question Book.

"The National Question Book." A graded course of study for those preparing to teach. By EDWARD R. SHAW, Principal of the High School, Yonkers, N. Y.; author of "School Devices," etc. Bound in durable English buckram cloth, with beautiful side-stamp. 12mo, 350 pp. Price, $1.50 ; *net to teachers*, postpaid.

This work contains 6,000 Questions and Answers on 22 Different Branches of Study.

ITS DISTINGUISHING FEATURES.

1. It aims to make the teacher a BETTER TEACHER.

"How to Make Teaching a Profession" has challenged the attention of the wisest teacher. It is plain that to accomplish this the teacher must pass from the stage of a knowledge of the rudiments, to the stage of somewhat extensive acquirement. There are steps in this movement ; if a teacher will take the first and see what the next is, he will probably go on to the next, and so on. One of the reasons why there has been no movement forward by those who have made this first step, is that there was nothing marked out as a second step.

2. This book will show the teacher how to go forward.

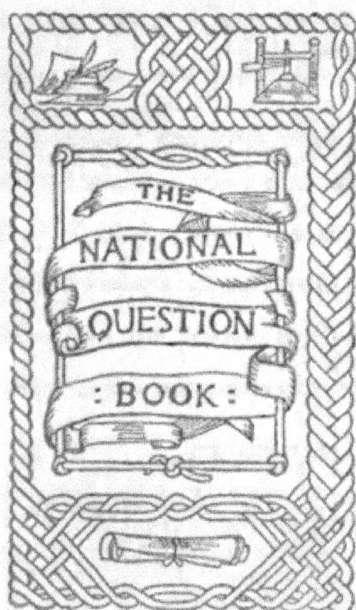

In the preface the course of study usually pursued in our best normal schools is given. This proposes four grades: third, second, first, and professional. Then, questions are given appropriate for each of these grades. Answers follow each section. A teacher will use the book somewhat as follows :— If he is in the third grade he will put the questions found in this book concerning numbers, geography, history, grammar, orthography, and theory and practice of teaching to himself and get out the answer. Having done this he will go on to the other grades in a similar manner. In this way he will know as to his fitness to pass an examination for these grades.   The selection of questions is a good **one.**

3. It proposes questions concerning teaching itself.
The need of studying the Art of Teaching is becoming more
and more apparent.   There are questions that will prove very
suggestive and valuable on the Theory and Practice of Education.

4. It is a general review of the common **school** and higher
studies.

Each department of questions is followed by department of
answers on same subject, each question being numbered, and
answer having corresponding number.

Arithmetic, 3d grade.	English Literature, 1st grade.
Geography, 2d and 3d grade.	Natural Philosophy, "
U. S. History, 2d and 3d grade.	Algebra, professional grade.
Grammar, 1st, 2d, and 3d grade.	General History, profess. grade.
Orthography and Orthoepy, 3d grade.	Geometry, " "
Theory and Practice of Teaching,	Latin, " "
1st, 2d, and 3d grade.	Zoology, " "
Rhetoric and Composition, 2d grade.	Astronomy, " "
Physiology, 1st and 2d grade.	Botany, " "
Bookkeeping, 1st and 2d grade.	Physics.
Civil Government, 1st and 2d grade.	Chemistry, " "
Physical Geography, 1st grade.	Geology, " "

5. It is carefully graded into grades corresponding to those
into which teachers are usually classed.

It is important for a teacher to know what are appropriate
questions to ask a third grade teacher, for example.   Examiners of teachers, too, need to know what are appropriate
questions.   In fact, to put the examination of the teacher into
a proper system is most important.

6. Again, this book broadens the field, and will advance
education.   The second grade teacher, for example, is examined in rhetoric and composition, physiology, book-keeping,
and civil government, subjects usually omitted.   The teacher
who follows this book faithfully will become as near as possible a *normal school graduate.*   It is really a contribution to
pedagogic progress.   It points out to the teacher a *road to
professional fitness.*

7. It **is a** useful reference work for every teacher and private library.

Every teacher needs a book to turn to for questions, for
example, a history class.   Time is precious ; he gives a pupil
the book saying, " Write five of those questions on the blackboard ; the class **may** bring in answers to-morrow."   A book,

made on the broad principles this is, has numerous uses.

8. Examiners of teachers will find it especially valuable. It represents the standard required in New York and the East generally for third, second, first, and state diploma grades. It will tend to make a uniform standard throughout the United States.

WHAT IS SAID OF IT.

A Great Help.—"It seems to be well adapted to the purposes for which it is prepared. It will undoubtedly be a great help to many teachers who are preparing to pass an examination."—E. A. GASTMAN, Supt. Schools, Decatur, Ill.

Very Suggestive.—"I consider it very suggestive. As a book for class-room use it can serve a very important object by this suggestiveness, which is the peculiar quality of the book. Many of the questions suggest others to the teacher, and thus open her mind to new aspects of the book she is teaching. Such questions aid pupils in looking up matter which they have previously acquired, and yet supply the charm of novelty."—B. C. GREGORY, Secretary of N. J. Reading Circle.

Helpful to Young Teachers.—"It will prove a helpful book to young teachers who wish to review the studies which it treats."—T. M. BAILLIET, Supt. Schools, Springfield, Mass.

Well Fitted for its Purpose.—"I find it well fitted for its purpose in testing the acquaintance of students with the principles that govern the several departments of science and their application to special cases. I can see how a teacher can make good use of this book in his classes."—D. L. KIEHLE, Supt. of Public Instruction, St. Paul, Minn.

Without a Peer.—"It is without a peer."—J. M. GREENWOOD, Supt Schools, Kansas City, Mo.

Best for its Price.—"It is the best book for its price that I ever purchased."—MISS EVA QUIGLEY, teacher at La Porte, Cal.

Best of the Kind.—"It is decidedly the best book of the kind I ever examined."—D. G. WILLIAMS, Ex-Co. Supt. York County, Pa.

Will Furnish Valuable Ideas.—"It presents a larger variety than usual of solid questions. Will repay very largely all efforts put forth by examiners and examined, and lead to better work in the several branches. The questions have been carefully studied. They are the result of thoughtful experience, and will furnish valuable ideas."—CHAS JACOBUS, Supt. Schools, New Brunswick, N. J.

J. H. Hoose, Prin. of the Cortland (N. Y.) Normal School, says:—"It will be helpful to those persons who cannot enjoy an attendence upon courses of study in some good school."

Hon. B. G. Northrup, of Connecticut, says:—"It is at once concise and comprehensive, *stimu ati g* and instructive. These questions seem to show the young teacher what he d *es not know* and ought to know and facilitates the acquisition of the desired knowledge."

School Education (Minn.) says:—"Many a young teacher of good mind, whose opportunities have been meagre, and who does not yet know how to study effectively in a scientific spirit, may be stimulated to look up points, and to genuine progress in self-improvement by such a book as this. The questions are systematically arranged, worded with judgment, and are accompanied by numerous analyses of various subjects."

Payne's Lectures on the Science and

ART OF EDUCATION. *Reading Circle Edition.* By JOSEPH
PAYNE, the first Professor of the Science and Art of Education in the College of Preceptors, London, England.
With portrait. 16mo, 350 pp., English cloth, with gold
back stamp. Price, $1.00 ; *to teachers,* 80 cents ; by mail,
7 cents extra. *Elegant new edition from new plates.*

Teachers who are seeking to
know the principles of education
will find them clearly set forth in
this volume. It must be remembered that principles are the basis
upon which all methods of teaching must be founded. So valuable is this book that if a teacher
were to decide to own but three
works on education, this would
be one of them. This edition
contains all of Mr. Payne's writ-
ings that are in any other American abridged edition, and *is the
only one with his portrait.* It is
far superior to any other edition
published.

JOSEPH PAYNE.

WHY THIS EDITION IS THE BEST.

(1.) The *side-titles.* These give the contents of the page.
(2.) The analysis of each lecture, with reference to the *educational* points in it. (3.) The general analysis pointing out the
three great principles found at the beginning. (4.) The index,
where, under such heads as Teaching, Education, The Child,
the important utterances of Mr. Payne are set forth. (5.)
Its handy shape, large type, fine paper, and press-work and
tasteful binding. All of these features make this a most valuable book. To obtain all these features in one edition, it
was found necessary to *get out this new edition.*

Ohio Educational Monthly.—"It does not deal with shadowy theories :
it is intensely practical."
Philadelphia Educational News.—"Ought to be in library of every
progressive teacher."
Educational Courant.—"To know how to teach, more is needed than
a knowledge of the branches taught. This is especially valuable."
Pennsylvania Journal of Education.—"Will be of practical value to
Normal Schools and Institutes."

Shaw and Donnell's School Devices.

"School Devices." A book of ways and suggestions for teachers. By EDWARD R. SHAW and WEBB DONNELL, of the High School at Yonkers, N. Y. Illustrated. Dark-blue cloth binding, gold, 16mo, 224 pp. Price, $1.25 ; *to teachers*, $1.00 ; by mail, 9 cents extra.

☞ **A BOOK OF "WAYS" FOR TEACHERS.**

Teaching **is an** art ; there are "ways to do **it**." This book is made to point out "ways," and to help by suggestions.

1. It gives "ways" for teaching Language, Grammar, **Reading**, Spelling, Geography, etc. These are in many cases novel ; they are designed to help attract the attention of the pupil.

2. The "ways" given are not **the** questionable "ways" so **often** seen practiced in school-rooms, but are in accord **with** the spirit of modern educational ideas.

3. This book will afford practical assistance to teachers who wish to keep their work from degenerating into mere routine. It gives them, in convenient form for constant use at the desk, a multitude of new ways in **which** to present old truths. The great enemy of the teacher is want of interest. Their methods do not attract attention. There is no teaching unless there **is** *attention*. The teacher is too apt to think there is but one "way" of teaching spelling ; he thus falls **into a rut. Now** there are **many** "ways" of teaching spelling, **and** some "ways" are better than others. Variety **must** exist **in** the school-room ; the authors of this volume deserve the thanks of the teachers for pointing **out** methods of obtaining variety without sacrificing the great end sought—scholarship. New "ways" induce greater effort, and renewal of activity.

4. The book gives the result of large actual experience in the school-room, and will meet the needs of thousands of teachers, by placing at their command that for which visits to other schools are made, institutes and associations attended, viz., new ideas and fresh and forceful ways of teaching. The devices given under Drawing and Physiology **are** of an eminently practical nature, and cannot fail to invest these subjects with new interest. The attempt has been made to present only devices of a practical character.

5. The book suggests "ways" to make teaching *effective ;* it is not simply a book of new "ways," but of "ways" that will produce good results.

WHAT IT CONTAINS.

"Ways" **of** teaching Language—Geography—Spelling—Reading—Arithmetic — History — Physiology — Drawing—Penmanship—Personal Suggestions—School-Room Suggestions—Outside the School-Room—Seat Work. The first chapter on *Language* contains: A Way to Prepare Pictures for Young Pupils—Supplying the Proper Word—A Language Lesson—Weekly Plan of Language Work for Lower Grammar Grades—Writing Ordinals—Correcting Bad English—For Beginners in Composition—Word Developing—An Easy Exercise in Composition—Composition from Pictures—Plan for Oral Composition—Debating Exercises—Language Drill in every Lesson—Letter Writing—Matter for Letters—Forms for Business Letters—Papers Written from Recitation Notes—Equivalent Forms of Expression—Devices for Use of Capitals—Excerpts to Write Out from Memory—Regular Plan in Composition Writing—To Exercise the Imagination—Suggestions about Local Subjects for Compositions—A Letter Written upon the Blackboard by all the Class—Choice of Words—Order of Criticism—A Plan for Rapid Correction of Compositions—To File and Hold Essays—Assigning a Subject for a Composition—Character Sketches—Illustrative Syntax—A Talk on Language —A Grammar Lesson, Device for Building up the Conjugation of the Verb—The Infinitive Mood—Shall and Will—Matter for a Talk on Words —Surnames.

At the end of the volume is inserted a careful selection of Bible Readings for every school day of the year, with the pronunciation of difficult words—a provision that will be appreciated by those who are obliged to hunt each morning for a proper selection for school devotions.

Mr. E. R. Shaw, of the Yonkers High School, is well known, and Mr. Webb Donnell, of the East Machias (Me.) Academy, is a teacher of fine promise ; they have put together a great variety **of** suggestions that cannot fail to be of real service.

Home and School.—"Is just the book for every teacher who wishes to be a better teacher."

Educational Journal.—"It contains many valuable hints."

Boston Journal of Education.—"It is the most humane, instructive, original educational work we have read in many a day."

Wis. Journal of Education.—"Commends itself at once by the number of ingenious devices for securing order, industry, and interest."

Iowa Central School Journal.—"Teachers will find it a helpful and suggestive book."

Canada Educational Monthly.—"Valuable advice and useful suggestions."

Normal Teacher.—"The author believes the way to manage is to civilize, cultivate, and refine."

School Moderator.—"Contains a large amount of valuable reading. School government is admirably presented."

Progressive Teacher.—"Should occupy an honored place in every teacher's library."

Ed. Courant.—"It will help the teacher greatly."

Va. Ed. Journal.—"The author draws from a large experience."

Country and Village Schools.—"Cannot fail to be serviceable."

Patridge's " Quincy Methods."

The " Quincy Methods," illustrated ; Pen photographs from
the Quincy schools. By Lelia E. Patridge. Illustrated
with a number of engravings, and two colored plates.
Blue **cloth**, gilt, 12mo, 686 pp. Price, $1.75 ; *to teachers,*
$1.40 ; **by** mail, 13 cents extra.

When **the** schools of Quincy, Mass., became so famous
under **the** superintendence of Col. Francis W. Parker, thousands **of** teachers visited them. Quincy became a sort of
"educational Mecca," to the disgust of the routinists, whose
schools were passed by. Those who went to study the
methods pursued there were called on to tell what they had
seen. Miss Patridge was one of those who visited the schools
of Quincy ; in the Pennsylvania Institutes (many of which
she conducted), she found the teachers were never tired of
being told how things were done in Quincy. She revisited
the schools several times, and wrote down what she saw ; then
the book was made.

1. This book presents the actual practice in the schools of
Quincy. It is composed of " pen photographs."

2. It gives abundant reasons for the great stir produced by
the two words " Quincy Methods." There are reasons for the
discussion that has been going on among the teachers of late
years.

3. It gives **an** insight to principles underlying real education as distinguished from book learning.

4. It shows the teacher not only what to do, but gives the
way in which to do it.

5. It impresses one with **the** *spirit* of the Quincy schools.

6. It shows the teacher how to create an *atmosphere* of hap-
piness, of busy work, and of progress.

7. It shows the teacher how not to waste her time in worry-
ing **over** disorder.

8. It tells how **to treat pupils** with courtesy, and get courtesy back again.

9. It presents four years of work, considering Number,
Color, Direction, Dimension, Botany, Minerals, Form, Lan-
guage, Writing, Pictures, Modelling, Drawing, Singing,
Geography, Zoology, etc., etc.

10. There are 686 pages; a large book devoted to the realities
of school life, in realistic descriptive language. It is plain,
real, not abstruse and uninteresting.

11. It gives an insight into real education, the education
urged by Pestalozzi, Frœbel, Mann, Page, Parker, etc.

12. It exemplifies the teachings of Col. F. W. Parker in the "Talks on Teaching." It must be remembered that the "Talks" were from the notes taken by Miss Patridge, the author of this book. To understand what the teaching is that Col. Parker would have in the schools, one must read this book, or attend his school at Normal Park, Ill.

Pa. School Journal:—"The book will be of historical significance." **N. Y. School Bulletin:**—"Should be one of the first dozen books in the teacher's library." **Boston Journal of Education:**—"Affords a clear insight into the methods and work at Quincy." **Iowa Teacher:**—"The best of it is that the underlying principles are explained." **Chicago Practical Teacher:**—"Miss Patridge has done her work thoroughly and well." **N. C. Teacher:**—"The story of the Quincy method is well told." **La. School Journal:**—"The work ought to be in every public school library." **Chicago Intelligence:**—"It is really a manual for the primary teacher." **Teachers' Quarterly:**—"Beautifully told in this volume." **Cincinnati School Journal:**—"The book explains the underlying principles." **S. W. Journal of Education:**—"Miss Patridge has done the work excellently well." **Indiana School Bulletin:**—"Full of good suggestions." **Pa. Teacher:**—"No teacher can read it without receiving ideas and helpful suggestions." **Pa. School Journal:**—"This book has a mission." **Nat. (Pa.) Educator:**—"Every progressive teacher will get more benefit from it than from any other published." **Our County and Village Schools:**—"Reading this volume will produce a revolution." **Ed. Courant:**—"Has the power, fervor, and style of Parker." **Wis. Journal of Education:**—"By far the most complete manual of the 'New Education." **Ill. School Journal:**—"It is without question the fullest, richest, and most suggestive volume for grade teachers, and also for superintendents, that it has been our portion to examine." **Normal Exponent:**—"Every teacher should read it." **W. Va. School Journal:**—"It is a fountain from which new and refreshing draughts may be drawn." **Philadelphia Teacher:**—"Abounds with hints; will prove a precious guide." **Chicago Advance:**—"In the presence of such a book we pause with reverence." **School Education:**—"Is a very desirable book." **Phrenological Journal:**—"It is the application of principles." **Christian Advocate:**—"Well worth the perusal of teachers." **Texas School Journal:**—"No primary teacher can afford to do without this work." **Springfield Republican:**—"The earnest teacher will find it helpful." **Quebec Ed. Record:**—"Pleased that it is on the list of books for teachers." **The Critic:**—"Gives a helpful insight into the theory of Education." **Interior:**—"Well worthy of study." **Interocean:**—"One of the books that should be found in every teacher's desk." **Detroit Free Press:**—Will take a high place in educational literature." **S. S. Times:**—"First and best for the Sunday school teacher is **Quincy Methods.**"

Tate's Philosophy of Education.

The Philosophy of Education. By T. TATE. Revised and Annotated by E. E. SHEIB, Ph.D., Principal of the Louisiana State Normal School. Unique cloth binding, laid paper, 331 pp. Price, $1.50; *to teachers*, $1.20; by mail, 7 cents extra.

There **are few** books that deal with the Science of Education. This **volume is** the work of a man who said there were great principles at the bottom of the work of the despised schoolmaster. It has set many a teacher to thinking, and in its new form will set many more.

Our edition will be found far superior to any other in every respect. The annotations of Mr. Sheib are invaluable. The more important part of the book are emphasized by leading the type. The type is clear, the size convenient, and printing, paper, and binding are most excellent.

Mr. Philbrick so long superintendent of the Boston schools hold this work in high esteem.

Col. F. W. Parker strongly recommends it.

Jos. MacAlister, Supt. Public Schools, Philadelphia, says:—"It is one of the first books which a teacher deserves of understanding the scientific principles on which his work rests should study."

S. A. Ellis, Supt. of Schools, Rochester N. Y. says:—"As a pointed and judicious statement of principles it has no superior."

Thos. M. Balliet, Supt. of Schools, Reading. Pa., says:—"The work is a classic on Education."

J. M. Greenwood, Supt. Schools, Kansas City, says:—"I wish every teacher of our country owned a copy and would read it carefully and thoughtfully."

Prest. E. A. Sheldon, Oswego Normal Schools, says:—"For more than 20 years it has been our text-book in this subject and I know of no other book so good for the purpose."

Bridgeport Standard.—"A new generation of thinkers will welcome it; it has long held the first place in the field of labor which it illustrates."

S. W. Journal of Education.—"It deals with fundamental principles and shows how the best educational practice comes from them."

The Interior.—"The book has long been held in high esteem by thoughtful teachers."

Popular Educator.—"Has long held a high place among educational works."

Illinois School Journal.—"It abounds in good things."

Philadelphia Record.—"Has been ranked among educational classics for more than a quarter of a century."

Educational News.—"Tate was the first to give us the maxims from the 'known to the unknown' etc."

The Reading Circle Library.

No. 1. Allen's Mind Studies for Young Teachers

By JEROME ALLEN, Ph.D., Associate Editor of the SCHOOL JOURNAL, formerly President of the St. Cloud (Minn.) Normal School. 16mo, large, clear type; 128 pp. paper cover. Price, 30 cents; *to teachers,* 24 cents; by mail, 3 cents extra. Limp cloth, 50 cents; *to teachers,* 40 cents; by mail, 5 cents extra. *Special rates for quantities.* Fourth thousand now ready.

This little volume attempts to open the subject of Psychology in a plain way, omitting what is abstruse and difficult. It is written in language easily comprehended, and has practical illustrations. It will be wanted by teachers.

1. Some knowledge of Mental Science is indispensible to the teacher. He is dealing with Perception, Attention, Judgment. He ought to know what these mean.

2. The relation between Teaching and Mind Growth is pointed out; it is not a dry treatise on Psychology.

3. It is a work that will aid the teacher in his daily work in dealing with mental facts and states.

Popular Educator.—"The teacher will find **in it much** information as well as incitement to thought."

Jared Sanford, School Com., Mt. Vernon, N. Y.—"From all points of view it must prove of great worth to those who read it. To the earnest teacher in search of information concerning the principles of Psychology it **is** to be highly commended."

Irwin Shepard, Pres. Normal School, Winona, Minn.—"I am much pleased with it. It certainly fills a want. Most teachers need a smaller briefer, and more convenient Manual than has before been issued."

S. G. Love, Supt. School, N. Y.—"I want to say of it that it is an excellent little book. Invaluable for building up the young teacher in that kind of knowledge indispensable to successful teaching to-day."

Prof. Edward Brooks.—"The work **will** be very useful to young teachers."

No. 2.   Autobiography of Frœbel.

Materials to Aid a Comprehension of the Works of the
Founder of the Kindergarten. 16mo, large, clear type,
128 pp. Unique paper cover. Price, 30 cents; *to
teachers*, 24 cents; by mail, 8 cents extra. Bound in limp
cloth, 50 cents; *to teachers*, 40 cents; by mail, 5 cents
extra.

This little volume will be welcomed by all who want to get
a good idea of Frœbel and the kindergarten.

FRIEDRICH FRŒBEL.

1. The dates connected with
Frœbel and the kindergarten
are given, then follows his
autobiography. To this is
added Joseph Payne's estimate and portrayal of Frœbel, as well as a summary of
Frœbel's own views.

2. In this volume the student of education finds materials for constructing, in an
intelligent manner an estimate
and comprehension of the kindergarten. The life of Frœbel,
mainly by his own hand, is
very helpful. In this we see
the working of his mind when
a youth; he lets us see how
he felt at being misunder-
stood, at being called a bad boy, and his pleasure when face
to face with nature. Gradually we see there was crystallizing
in him a comprehension of the means that would bring har-
mony and peace to the minds of young people.

3. The analysis of the powers of Frœbel will be of great
aid. We see that there was a deep philosophy in this plain
German man; he was studying out a plan by which the
usually wasted years of young children could be made pro-
ductive. The volume will be of great value not only to every
kindergartner, but to all who wish to understand the philosophy of mental development.

La. Journal of Education.—" An excellent little work.'

W. Va. School Journal.—" Will be of great value."

Educational Courant, Ky.—" Ought to have a very extensive circu-
lation among the teachers of the country."

Educational Record, Can.—" Ought to be in the hands of every professional teacher."

No. 3.   Hughes' Mistakes in Teaching.

By JAMES L. HUGHES, Inspector of Schools, Toronto, Canada. Cloth, 16mo, 115 pp. Price, 50 cents ; *to teachers*, 40 cents ; by mail, 5 cents extra.

Thousands of copies of the old edition have been sold.. The new edition is worth double the old ; the material has been increased, restated and greatly improved. Two new and important Chapters have been added on " Mistakes in Aims," and " Mistakes in Moral Training." Mr. Hughes says in his preface : " In issuing a revised edition of this book it seems fitting to acknowledge gratefully the hearty appreciation that has been accorded it by

JAMES L. HUGHES.

American teachers. Realizing as I do that its very large sale indicates that it has been of service to many of my fellow teachers, I have recognized the duty of enlarging and revising it so as to make it still more helpful in preventing the common mistakes in teaching and training."

Ninety-Six important mistakes are corrected in this book. This is the only edition authorized by the writer.

The Schoolmaster (England)—"His ideas are clearly presented."

Boston Journal of Education.—" Mr. Hughes evidences a thorough study of the philosophy of education. We advise every teacher to invest 50 cents in the purchase of this useful volume."

New York School Journal.—"It will help any teacher to read this book."

Chicago Educational Weekly.—"Only long experience could furnish the author so fully with materials for sound advice."

Penn. Teacher's **Advocate.**—" It is the most readable book we have seen lately."

Educational Journal of Virginia.—" We know no book that contains so many valuable suggestions."

Ohio Educational Monthly.—"It contains more practical hints than any book of its size known to us."

Iowa Central School Journal.—"We know of no book containing more valuable suggestions."

New York School Bulletin—" It is sensible and practical."

No. 4. Hughes' Securing and Retaining Attention.

By JAMES L. HUGHES, Inspector Schools, Toronto, Canada. Author of Mistakes in Teaching. Cloth, 116 pp. Price, 50 cents ; *to teachers*, 40 cents ; by mail, 5 cents extra.

This **valuable little** book has already become widely known to American **teachers.** This new edition has been almost entirely re-**written** and several new important chapters added. It is the only edition authorized by the author. The testimonials to the old edition are more than deserved for the new one.

Educational Times. England.—"On an important subject, and admirably executed."

School Guardian. England.—"We unhesitatingly recommend it."

New England Journal of Education.—"The book is a guide and a manual of special value."

New York School Journal.—"Every teacher would derive benefit **from** reading this volume."

Chicago Educational Weekly.—"The **teacher who aims at** best success should study it."

Phil. Teacher.—"Many who **have spent months in the school-room** would be benefitted by it."

Maryland School Journal.—"Always clear, never tedious."

Va. Ed..Journal.—"Excellent hints as to securing attention."

Ohio Educational Monthly.—"We advise readers to send for a copy."

Pacific Home and School Journal.—"An excellent little manual."

Prest. James H. Hoose, State Normal School, Cortland, N. Y., says :— "The book must prove of great benefit to the profession."

Supt. A. W. Edson, Jersey, City, N. J., says :—"A good treatise has long been needed, and Mr. Hughes has supplied the want."

No. 5. The Student's Calendar.

For 1888. Compiled by N. O. WILHELM. Elegant design on heavy cardboard, 9 x 11 inches, printed in gold and color. Price, 60 cts. ; *to teachers*, 48 cents. ; by mail, 8 cts. In book form, *for any year*, paper cover. Price, 30 cts. ; *to teachers*, 24 cts. ; by mail, 3 cts. extra.

This beautiful, novel, and useful calendar is designed to assist teachers in preparing exercises for MEMORIAL DAYS, and also to suggest topics for "talks," compositions, etc. The idea is entirely new. Opposite each date is a very short life of some great man who was born or died on that day. The design is superb, and printing, etc., tasteful and elegant, making it an ornament for any room.

Teachers' Manuals Series.

Each **is printed** in large, clear type, on good paper. Paper cover, price 15 cents; to teachers, 12 cents; by mail 1 cent extra. Liberal discount in quantities.

There is a **need of small** volumes —"E d u c a t i o n a l tracts," that teachers can carry easily and study as they have opportunity. The following six have been already selected. Every one is a gem. **To** call them the " Educational Gem" series would be more appropriate.

It should be noted that while our editions of these **little** books are as low in price as any other, the side heads, topics and analyses inserted **by** the editors, **as** well as the excellent paper and printing, make them far superior in every way to any other.

No. 1. FITCH'S ART **OF** QUESTIONING.
By J. G. FITCH, M. A., author of "Lectures on Teaching." 38 pp.
Already widely known as the most useful and practical essay **on** this most important part of the teachers' lesson-hearing.

No. 2. FITCH'S **ART** OF SECURING ATTENTION.
By **J. G.** FITCH, **M. A.,** 39 pp.
Of no less value **than** the author's **"Art of Questioning."**

No. 3. SIDGWICK'S ON STIMULUS **IN SCHOOL.**
By ARTHUR SIDGWICK, M. A. 43 pp.
"How can that dull, lazy scholar be pressed **on to work up his lessons** with a will." This bright essay will tell how **it can be done.**

No. 4. YONGE'S PRACTICAL WORK IN SCHOOL.
By CHARLOTTE M. YONGE, author of "Heir of Redclyffe." 35 pp.
All who have read Miss Yonge's books will be glad to read of her views on School Work.

No. 5. FITCH'S IMPROVEMENT IN THE ART OF TEACHING.
By J. G. FITCH, M. A. 25 pp.
This thoughtful, earnest essay will bring courage and help to many a teacher who is struggling to do better work. It includes a course of study for Teachers' Training Classes.

No. 6. GLADSTONE'S OBJECT TEACHING.
By J. H. GLADSTONE, of the London (Eng.) School Board. 25 pp.
A short manual full of practical suggestions on Object Teaching.

Reception Day. 6 Nos.

A collection of fresh and original dialogues, recitations, declamations, and short pieces for practical use in Public and Private Schools. Bound in handsome, new paper **cover, 160 pages** each, printed on laid paper. Price 30 **cents** each ; *to teachers,* 24 cents ; by mail, 3 cents extra.
The exercises in these books bear upon education ; have **a** relation to the school-room.

NEW COVER.

1. **The** dialogues, recitations, and declamations, gathered in this volume being fresh, short, easy to be comprehended and are well fitted for the average scholars of our schools.

2. They have mainly been used by teachers for actual school exercises.

3. They cover a different ground from the speeches of Demosthenes and Cicero—which are unfitted for boys of twelve to sixteen years of age.

4. They have some practical interest for those who **use** them.

5. There is not a vicious sentence uttered. In some dialogue books profanity is found, or disobedience to parents encouraged, **or** lying laughed at. Let teachers look out for this.

6. There is something for the youngest pupils.

7. " Memorial Day Exercises " for Bryant, Garfield, Lincoln, etc., will be found.

8. Several Tree Planting exercises are included.

9. The **exercises** have relation **to** the school-room and bear upon education.

10. An important point **is** the freshness of these pieces. Most of them were written expressly for this collection, and *can be found nowhere else.*

Boston Journal of Education.—"Is of practical value."
Detroit Free Press.—" Suitable for public and private schools."
Western Ed. Journal.—" A series of very **good** selections."

www.ingramcontent.com/pod-product-compliance
Lightning Source LLC
Chambersburg PA
CBHW021554270326
41931CB00009B/1207